NORTH AMERICAN ANIMALS
Raccoons

by Chris Bowman

BLASTOFF! READERS

3

Note to Librarians, Teachers, and Parents:

Blastoff! Readers are carefully developed by literacy experts and combine standards-based content with developmentally appropriate text.

Level 1 provides the most support through repetition of high-frequency words, light text, predictable sentence patterns, and strong visual support.

Level 2 offers early readers a bit more challenge through varied simple sentences, increased text load, and less repetition of high-frequency words.

Level 3 advances early-fluent readers toward fluency through increased text and concept load, less reliance on visuals, longer sentences, and more literary language.

Level 4 builds reading stamina by providing more text per page, increased use of punctuation, greater variation in sentence patterns, and increasingly challenging vocabulary.

Level 5 encourages children to move from "learning to read" to "reading to learn" by providing even more text, varied writing styles, and less familiar topics.

Whichever book is right for your reader, Blastoff! Readers are the perfect books to build confidence and encourage a love of reading that will last a lifetime!

This edition first published in 2016 by Bellwether Media, Inc.

No part of this publication may be reproduced in whole or in part without written permission of the publisher. For information regarding permission, write to Bellwether Media, Inc., Attention: Permissions Department, 5357 Penn Avenue South, Minneapolis, MN 55419.

Library of Congress Cataloging-in-Publication Data

Bowman, Chris, 1990-
  Raccoons / by Chris Bowman.
     pages cm. – (Blastoff! Readers. North American Animals)
Summary: "Simple text and full-color photography introduce beginning readers to raccoons. Developed by literacy experts for students in kindergarten through third grade"– Provided by publisher.
  Audience: Ages 5-8
  Audience: K to grade 3
  Includes bibliographical references and index.
  ISBN 978-1-62617-263-0 (hardcover: alk. paper)
  1. Raccoon–Juvenile literature. I. Title.
  QL737.C26B69 2016
  599.76'32–dc23
                                                        2014050317

Table of
Contents

What Are Raccoons?

Raccoons are **mammals** found throughout North America.

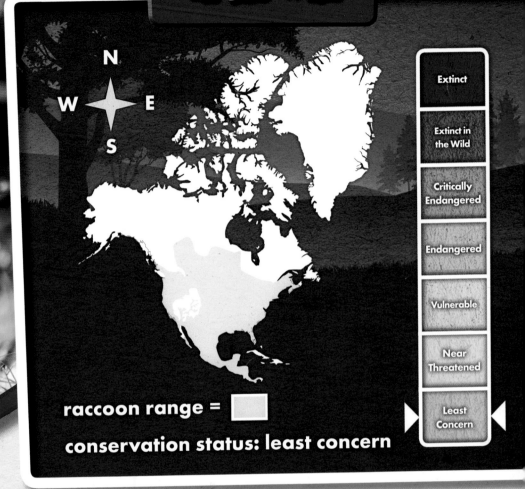

N
W E
S

Extinct

Extinct in the Wild

Critically Endangered

Endangered

Vulnerable

Near Threatened

Least Concern

raccoon range =

conservation status: least concern

They live in forests and grasslands from Canada to Panama. Some even call cities home.

Most raccoons like to be near water. They build homes called **dens**.

These are often in trees, logs, or unused **burrows**. Dens can also be in old buildings.

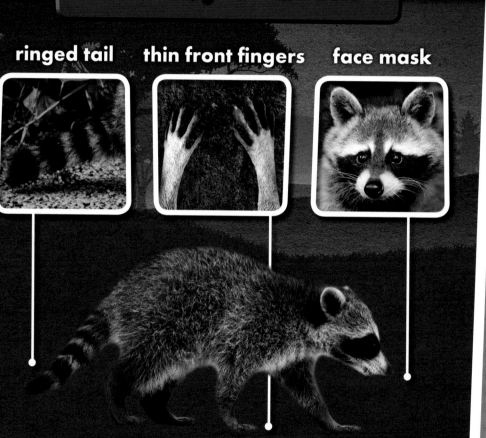

ringed tail   thin front fingers   face mask

Raccoons have gray, brown, or yellow fur. They are known for their ringed tails and mask-like markings.

They also have pointed noses, short ears, and short legs. Their front paws have long fingers with sharp claws.

Finding Food

Raccoons use their front paws to **grip** food. These **omnivores** eat anything available.

acorns

corn

crayfish

wood frogs

deer mice

spur-throated
grasshoppers

They **forage** for fruits, seeds,
and bird eggs. They also hunt fish,
insects, and **rodents**. Many even
eat out of human trash cans.

11

In the north, food can be hard
to find in the coldest months.

Raccoons in these areas eat as much as they can during summer and fall. Then they sleep for much of winter.

Boars, Sows, and Cubs

Male raccoons are called **boars**. They are bigger than females, or **sows**.

Size of a Raccoon

average human

raccoon

6
5
4
3
2
1
(feet)

They grow to be about 24 to 42 inches (61 to 107 centimeters) long. Most boars weigh between 8 and 23 pounds (3.6 and 10.4 kilograms).

coyotes

great horned owls

gray wolves

mountain lions

bobcats

red foxes

Their large size often keeps **predators** from attacking. When danger is near, raccoons hiss, bark, and growl.

Their sharp teeth also help fight off snakes, **raptors**, and other large animals.

Sows give birth to **cubs** in spring or summer. **Newborn** raccoons are blind. Their eyes open after about three weeks. Mom stays near to protect her cubs.

Baby Facts

Names for babies:	cubs or kits
Size of litter:	1 to 7 cubs
Length of pregnancy:	2 months
Time spent with mom:	1 year

19

After about two months,
raccoon cubs leave the den.
They search for food with mom.

They share her den for the next winter. Then they are ready to live on their own!

Glossary

boars—male raccoons

burrows—holes or tunnels that animals dig for homes

cubs—baby raccoons

dens—sheltered places; raccoons build dens in trees, logs, or in the ground.

forage—to go out in search of food

grip—to hold tightly

mammals—warm-blooded animals that have backbones and feed their young milk

newborn—just recently born

omnivores—animals that eat both plants and animals

predators—animals that hunt other animals for food

raptors—large birds that hunt other animals; raptors have excellent eyesight and powerful talons.

rodents—small animals that gnaw on their food

sows—female raccoons

To Learn More

AT THE LIBRARY

Johnson, J. Angelique. *Raccoons*. Mankato, Minn.: Capstone Press, 2011.

Petrie, Kristin. *Raccoons*. Minneapolis, Minn.: ABDO Publishing, 2015.

Read, Tracy C. *Exploring the World of Raccoons*. Buffalo, N.Y.: Firefly Books, 2010.

ON THE WEB

Learning more about raccoons is as easy as 1, 2, 3.

1. Go to www.factsurfer.com.

2. Enter "raccoons" into the search box.

3. Click the "Surf" button and you will see a list of related web sites.

With factsurfer.com, finding more information is just a click away.

Index

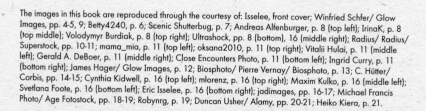

The images in this book are reproduced through the courtesy of: Isselee, front cover; Winfried Schfer/ Glow Images, pp. 4-5, 9; Betty4240, p. 6; Scenic Shutterbug, p. 7; Andreas Alfenburger, p. 8 (top left); IrinaK, p. 8 (top middle); Volodymyr Burdiak, p. 8 (top right); Ultrashock, pp. 8 (bottom), 16 (middle right); Radius/ Radius/ Superstock, pp. 10-11; mama_mia, p. 11 (top left); oksana2010, p. 11 (top right); Vitalii Hulai, p. 11 (middle left); Gerald A. DeBoer, p. 11 (middle right); Close Encounters Photo, p. 11 (bottom left); Ingrid Curry, p. 11 (bottom right); James Hager/ Glow Images, p. 12; Biosphoto/ Pierre Vernay/ Biosphoto, p. 13; C. Hütter/ Corbis, pp. 14-15; Cynthia Kidwell, p. 16 (top left); mlorenz, p. 16 (top right); Maxim Kulko, p. 16 (middle left); Svetlana Foote, p. 16 (bottom left); Eric Isselee, p. 16 (bottom right); jadimages, pp. 16-17; Michael Francis Photo/ Age Fotostock, pp. 18-19; Robynrg, p. 19; Duncan Usher/ Alamy, pp. 20-21; Heiko Kiera, p. 21.